NATIONAL
GEOGRAPHIC

People Who Lead Us

Lesley Pether

What is a leader?

A leader shows people how to do things.
Leaders help people work together as a team.

**Mr. Young is a
basketball coach.**

Mr. Young teaches the
players how to play basketball.
He teaches players the rules of the game.
He also shows them how to play as a team.

4

**Mrs. Lin is the
principal of
a school.**

Mrs. Lin works with
the teachers in the school.
She helps them get the materials they need.
She also helps them work together as a team.

**Mr. Sampson is
a scout troop
leader.**

Mr. Sampson shows the
scouts how to put up tents.
He teaches the scouts how to build campfires.
He also teaches them to work together as a team.

8

9

**Ms. Martino
is an orchestra
conductor.**

Ms. Martino leads all the
musicians in the orchestra.
She tells the musicians how to play the music.
She also helps them play together as a team.

Index